HISTORY IN BONES

HISTORY IN BONES

Juliana Gray Vice

The Kent State University Press
Kent & London

For my teachers

Library of Congress Catalog Card Number 2001007201
ISBN 0-87338-731-7
Manufactured in the United States of America

06 05 04 03 02   5 4 3 2 1

The Wick Poetry Chapbook Series is sponsored by the Stan and Tom Wick
Poetry Program and the Department of English at Kent State University.

Library of Congress Cataloging-in-Publication Data
Vice, Juliana Gray, 1972–
    History in bones / Juliana Gray Vice.
        p.   cm.—(Wick poetry chapbook ser. 2; no. 11)
    ISBN 0-87338-731-7 (pbk.: alk paper) ∞
    I. Title.   II. Wick poetry chapbook series; ser. 2, no. 11.

PS3622.I28 H57   2002
811'.6—dc21   2001007201

British Library Cataloging-in-Publication data are available.

CONTENTS

ACKNOWLEDGMENTS

Grateful acknowledgement is made to the publications in which earlier versions of the following poems appeared: *Alabama Literary Review:* "Noccalula Falls"; *New Delta Review:* "Here there be monsters"; and *Sewanee Theological Review:* "Speaking for the Moon."

I am also grateful for the suggestions and support of many friends, family, and teachers. I owe special thanks to the professors, workshop leaders, and editors who helped me bring this collection to life: Andrew Hudgins, Don Bogen, John Drury, Erin McGraw, Wyatt Prunty, Rodney Jones, Dave Smith, Robert Hass, Arthur Smith, Marilyn Kallett, Thomas Rabbitt, and Maggie Anderson. Thanks to everyone at the Sewanee Writers' Conference, especially Cheri Peters, Phil Stephens, Greg Williamson, Danny Anderson, Leah Stewart, Leigh Anne Couch, Liz Van Hoose, Ron Briggs, Kevin Wilson, and Heather Prunty. Thanks and much love to my friends, including Jim Murphy, Cynthia Nitz Ris, Lynn Shaffer, Gary Leising, Cate Marvin, and especially my husband Brad, for their criticism, encouragement and friendship. And finally, I wish to thank my parents for giving me the freedom to do what I love.

I

HERE THERE BE MONSTERS

Here is destiny, marked out in the hand:
rough calluses or none, nails sculptured
or bitten, the swelling of knuckles,
lines in the palm. Scarring, too,
is taken into account. All flesh is relevant.

A man with two hooks leering from his sleeves
is cursed above all men. He wakes to sighing metal,
the scrape of icebergs shifting at sea.
When a ghost hand itches in featureless dreams,
one memory reaches to scratch the other.

I know enough of palmistry
to read the wrongness of my lines,
the lifeline snapped midway,
resumed and deeply forked,
two wrinkled children, the erratum
of a freckle below the middle finger.
Saturn rules that finger, and the line of fate.
To read further is to be cursed with knowing.

BOTTLE IMP

The old apocalypse returns, recast
in modern forms: the smallpox virus coaxed
from Bangladeshi scabs and nurtured till
it fills its inch-long vials like ruined milk.

Does this feel familiar? Recognize it yet?
The virus, yes, but also the packaging,
the hackneyed bit about the genie trapped
inside the bottle—get the image now?

Familiar, yes, but it's meant to be. How else
are we supposed to know? Identify
refrigerated warheads by their skewed
trajectories, their top-heavy loll.

Identify the symptoms not by aches
and fever, not by pustules blooming red
as poppies, the skin's deliberate levitation
above the lower dermis—not by these,

but by the dreams which come before. The mind,
another genie, apprehends its fate
before the body registers a twinge,
and signals this in nightmares, images

of vague and crushing horror, indistinct
like dreams of infants overcome with sound
and heat and terrifying color—the signs
of one world ending, the next one looming dark.

But back to genies, the western term for djinn,
the demons roaming Arab wilderness
and desert, evil things which might allow
magicians to command them for a time—

invisible, they take the shape of bird
or beast or man, whatever suits them best—
a flea or viral corkscrew—each of these
is in their power, nestled deep in sand.

BERMAN MUSEUM OF MILITARY HISTORY, ANNISTON, ALABAMA

More rifles, pistols, flintlocks, muskets, carbines,
revolvers, daggers, sabers, bayonets,
scimitars, short swords, broadswords, spears,
crossbows, long bows, suits of armor, shells,
and medals than I could ever classify,
though Berman could. The collection filled his house
until he cut a deal with the town, loaded
fifty years' obsession, and brought it here.
Some is booty from the war, but most
he bought at auction, odd antiquities,
a rich man's toys. Upstairs is modern war,
below the ancient weaponry, most scuffed
and dented, some with gems still flashing bold
from hilts and scabbards. Mounted on the wall,
a Japanese beheading sword hangs
beside a photo Berman claimed he found
within an abandoned camera in Kagoshima—
a kneeling soldier in the street, his ruined face
caught as the blade divorces bone from bone.

In nearby cases rest more trophies, guns,
grenades, uncrumpled maps and uniforms,
badges, patches, snapshots of the dead.
Among it all, in over-lit display,
sits Adolf Hitler's silver tea service.
The cups, the pot, the saucers, sugar bowl
and spoons, the tiny pitcher for cream, the tray—
their surfaces gleam as bright as when their master
held them under Bavarian sunshine, stirred
his drink, and tapped the spoon against the rim
to hear the perfect tone. The light refracts
against engraved initials, spins out red
and green from the double-headed eagle's wings.
There's nothing here that surpasses it.

SPEAKING FOR THE MOON

You cannot comprehend this sky, unblemished
by stars. You cannot know the solemn ease
that settles after an age of pristine night:
no wind, no change, even the dust unstirred
for eons. I have the perfect solitude
of thought (though not what you would recognize
as thought), the choreography of earth
and sun, the dreams (you would not call them dreams)
of oceans. Madmen and lovers fall deranged
without my aid, imagine my waning face
is gazing down in sympathy. But I
am not concerned with this, with human love
or doleful sighs directed at the sky.
The graceful pull of waters, spring and neap,
the ebb and surge of surf over shore—
for these I spend my energies, for them
I wax and wane, seducing the mirrored waves.
It's not what you would recognize as love.

ANNISTON

Only when I moved to Tuscaloosa,
a hundred miles of pine and flowering scrub
from home, in a classroom choked with weary dust—
only then a Yankee teacher told me
a freedom rider bus was firebombed
in my home town. Our grade school books had skipped
from boll weevils to Werner Von Braun,
and Wallace was a god. But there it is:
in May of 1961, a group
of students, black and white, driving down
from Washington, D.C., was stopped outside
of Anniston. The white men forced them out
and beat them while the Greyhound roared in flames.
They beat them with chains. Or didn't. The men were Klan,
or town fathers, or a redneck gang from Georgia.
Perhaps there were two buses, and the beating came
in Birmingham. The single photograph
shows black students in white shirts sitting
on grass before the burned-out skeleton.
No landmarks dot the background—this could
be anywhere, but must be Highway 9,
or 431 down from Gadsden,
or 21, winding past the Fort,
or 78, the road I took to school,
where no one taught me this. But someone must
remember, must mark the spot when they drive past,
must notice how the kudzu's creeping up,
or how the extra lanes have paved it smooth
like frosting spooned atop a sunken cake.

Anniston began as Oxford Furnace,
smelting iron ore in the Civil War,
then lay abandoned till 1872,
when Tyler and Noble bought the rusting works,
renamed it Woodstock Furnace Company,
survived the Panic of 1873,

and incorporated Anniston. My books
tell me this much. I've played in Tyler Park
and shopped on Noble Street, and both men's graves
were well-kept sites for grade school pilgrimage.
At Christmastime, the streets downtown are hung
with countless ropes of tiny white lights,
and we'd drive down every block, past every store
that glimmered bright, admiring our pretty town.
The dirt in Anniston is blood-red clay,
too poor for cotton; no plantations rose
below Mount Cheaha, and slaves belonged
to other, richer lives further south.
But still that bus. But still that fire, those chains.
Our sorry clay is streaked with history's ash,
the only marker the town will still deny.

NOTES TOWARD AN ARS POETICA

A woman wakes. She rises, almost trips
over the cat entwined around her ankles.
The kitty mimics the percolator's drone.
The news recites the morning's catalog:
disasters from other hemispheres, the same
from hers, its housefires, earthquakes, names of the dead.

She showers, dresses, scrapes the early frost
from her windshield. Passing homes she can't afford,
she plans her day, the errands and household tasks.
A squirrel bounds into the road and freezes,
paralyzed between a forward flight
and retreat. She brakes and waits for it to choose.

In Produce, shaking water off bunches of kale,
she notes the price and smiles. "The kale's on sale,"
she whispers. A black woman tears a bag
from the spool and thumbs the plastic open, grins
and says, "Well, this must be our Christmas present!"

Selection is a kind of joy. She finds
a satisfaction, almost luxury,
in this bunch of scallions over that,
each box or can. There are no synonyms
among the brands; each carrot or garlic bulb
reveals to her its subtle properties.

And when the retarded bagboy drifts away
to follow the calls that only he can hear,
she steps around the cart and takes his place.
She keeps her eyes on her hands, tries not to stare
at the bagboy staring back across the store.

The kitchen work that evening eases her
toward rapture. Her heavy German knife is lovely
in her practiced hand. She often cuts herself,

but not tonight. The recipe instructs
a basil chiffonade, and she repeats
the word in rhythm with the rocking blade.

And everything—everything!—must
be tasted—the onions roasting in vinegar,
the pot of cream and wine simmering
with whole vanilla beans, the mushrooms, soft
and lush with butter. The flavors strike and meld,
the salt and spice, the alchemy of food.

But finally she has to deal with this,
the bitter heart of her creation, a lobster
stirring on the board. She bends to snip
the rubber bands around its claws and stops.
The recipe instructs the chef to drive the knife
between the flimsy plates behind its head,

rip off the tail and tear the claws away.
But should she ice it down to numb it first?
Or would the boiling water, just enough
to kindly kill it, change the taste so much?
The lobster shivers, slowly tries to walk.
How far will it get before she can decide?

The knife is balanced in her hand, and knows
it was made for cutting. Each decision counts.

CONVERGENCE AT THE KRISPY KREME

A large coffee and two glazed, hot off the conveyor
and glistening with sugar, cost $2.40.
I'm stirring in cream with a too-short straw,
trying not to burn my fingers, when two Canada geese
saunter past the window. Their curved bodies,
black and gray, balance on graceless feet.
How many vertebrae join in swiveling,
pivoting necks, spelling S, 2, 7, C,
beautiful lines not meant to be read?
The morning commuters steer around them,
easing from the drive-thru, one hand on the wheel,
one holding coffee, all eyes on the geese.
In the parking lot, five more, and the man
who bought a box of crullers says,
"I don't know what those ducks think they're doing,"
and looks like he's never been happier.
My coffee steams through its slotted lid.
We've all never been happier.

PIECES OF EIGHT

Learning history, it is easy to hate
the Spanish, for Cortés and De Soto,
for slavery and disease and the simple
discovery of an immaculate place.
Two hundred pounds of seed pearls,
Alabama's only treasure, were burned
in De Soto's battle at Maubilla,
a site still undiscovered, perhaps under
my town, my school, my own intruding feet.
What to make of this, of history
and how it engenders the present,
how the conquistadors decided
which pieces of Inca or Aztec artistry
to transport intact and which to melt down?
After the destruction of Maubilla,
Chief Tasçaluca's body could not be found.
History is easier piecemeal.
We take from it what we can.

II

BIRD, SMOKE, CRYSTAL, BONE

I.

The last December sunlight falls on these crows,
some four and twenty blackbirds scrabbling on snow,
their muddied beaks devouring crusts I'd left
for robins. Seen this close, through plate glass doors,
they're huge, as big as cats. The light won't shine,
reddened, from their black eyes. They bob their heads
obscenely till the chunks of bread go down.

Is there some augury in scavengers
who swerve from their nightly flight across the river
to roost in a Cincinnati graveyard, just
to steal the food of songbirds? Groups of crows
are called murders; rooks, a parliament.
Their cuneiform tracks reveal to the snow
its own defilement, rain that fell so soft
on gravestones, a drowning sailor's would-be breath,
the other incarnations of waters past.
Will I be able to read them? Ice has glazed
the snow beyond soft powder to gleaming chunks
that crunch and shatter under my boots. The crows
have left behind a feather, its rachis hot—
what bloody story would it tell for me?
Perhaps the truth for bread; perhaps a lie,
being crows. The bread wasn't mine, this house
not mine. The crows know they owe me nothing.

II.

This book I've pulled from a stranger's shelf,
an old, no doubt expensive leather-bound
on witchcraft, fails to mention New Year's Eve,
which seems an oversight. It's understood—
if only in the dour modern sense—
that this night is something magical.
Anticipation charges the air, the news,
and even the owners of this house have flown
to someplace elsewhere, better, to celebrate
in style. Their dog and I have gone through our
routines—just one more icy walk before
we call it a night. And in the meantime, this:
a few portentous hours to fill, to kill,
with pages falling open on their own,
the weight of print and plates and fissured spine
selecting for me passages to read,
a scattered history in bones and ash.

III.

The Romans favored augury, the tales
interpreted from flights of noble birds,
and gently unwound the shrouded blueprints of fate
from bulging entrails of sacrificed bulls.
They called this art haruspicy—each art,
however dark, must have an honest name.

The Druids read the death throes of victims bled
on sacred stones, and then, like Romans, turned
to viscera. Somewhere in those heavy coils,
the Druid and Roman priests divined each other,
the sacred groves destroyed, and Rome supreme—
and yet the Druids fought, their women and men
in holy black and blood-stained robes dead
and dying, their final prophecies fulfilled.

IV.

Such things are never easy. The smoke that curls
from sacred fires doesn't write itself
in English, won't spell out a word or name.
We look instead for faces, ashy ghosts
of war or love or fortune. Read them quickly,
before the wind can tear their shapes apart.

V.

Begin with artifacts, protected now
by inch-thick glass and velvet, under guard
at the British Museum. The book describes a slab
of rock, obsidian, and a crystal egg.
From this, take history: Hernán Cortés
at sail from savage Veracruz at last,
the mirror rock among his cargo of gold,
another trinket passed around at court
and later sent to woo the English bitch,
Elizabeth. Through her it came to Dee,
the court astrologer, an earnest man
who recognized his limits. He used
his Aztec magic glass for scrying, gazed
within its polished world until he found
some meaning, something to report to his Queen.
Dee knew he was no psychic, but kept his faith
in magic, even when his partner claimed
Madimi, the spirit from the crystal egg,
had ordered him and Dee to share their wives.
He trusted even this man, a charlatan
who'd lost his ears for forgery. They shared
reluctant wives, then broke their partnership.
Dee retired to his Mortlake house,
where enemies had burned or stolen books
and most of his scientific instruments.
His wife and daughter, Madimi, died of plague.
From his collection, three thousand books—
the *Stenographia,* Dee's response
the *Monas Hieroglyphia*—survived,
but only for display beside the egg
and clouded mirror, which, as Dee grew old
and destitute, and Elizabeth in her tomb,
would give him nothing but tricks of dimming light
and the meager-blossomed mist of his breath on stone.

VI.

Perhaps the girls discovered her at prayer—
exciting chants in the pantry's musty dark,
a pinch of flour on the fetish's leering mouth—
and threatened to tell the Reverend; perhaps
she led them willingly. Or Ann, the sole
surviving Putnam child, begged her help
to reach the children her mother still mourned.
Whatever the beginning, the end was this:
as Tituba cracked the egg in her hand, held back
the yolk in practiced fingers, and dropped the white
in a glass of swirling water, Abigail
and Ann and all the other Salem girls
leaned toward the future. Holding hands,
they studied the twisting proteins for signs
of husbands' occupations—Bible, plow,
or gavel.

    Tituba stood above them, lost
within the spell as coming months uncoiled:
the girls in fits, the Reverend's righteous fists,
confession of desperate lies, then thirteen months
of prison, chained to hold her spectre down—
awake in darkness, never again to see
Barbados—somehow saved from hanging, saved
for sale to a new master, seven pounds
to cover prison costs. Her history ends—
albumen settled on the bottom of the glass,
the yolk still dripped from Tituba's shaking hand.
The girls were waiting for more amusement. Now,
what choice but to conjure devils and confess?

VII.

The sun is down, the windows turned to mirrors
with the city lights behind. Myopic dots
of headlights trace the river, sweeping beams
of coal barges arching toward the shore.
The jingle of Gilda's collar carries down
the stairs to me, and the click of her nails like glass
on darkened tiles, the small noises of dogs.
She won't come down to watch TV with me.
She doesn't share my bourgeois tastes, is bored
by channel surfing (even though I skip
the Times Square revelry repeatedly);
perhaps she can't abide these late-night reels
of skin and cops and endless *M*A*S*H* repeats,
and psychics selling a glimpse of future fate.
They grin and sweat for authenticity,
parading testimonials of girls
in groups, ethnic and just a little trampy,
at malls and movie theaters, swearing truths:
My psychic said my grandma raised me—how
could she have known? She said my husband cheated,
and she was right. She knew my mother's name
was Frances.

            Is this their only offering,
a confirmation of the past? A cheap
biography of lying men, bad jobs,
forgotten family, and ruin, a voice
to understand, to say that fate absolves
their failures, empty flattery for sale
in prophecy's voice? The Sibyls never cared
to be loved. Entranced by smoke of green limbs,
burning moly twisted with hair, the women
spoke Apollo's words through raptured mouths,
regardless of what the seeker wished to hear.

When summoned, the witch at Cumae left her cave
and offered nine oracular volumes bound
with grape and olive vine, but Tarquinus Superbus,
the final king of Rome, refused her price.
She burned three volumes—still he would not pay.
She burned three more, and the king surrendered all
the fortune she had asked for the final three.
Tarquinus Superbus—had he paid her price
at first, we might still recognize his name.

VIII.

Were we so different from those Salem girls,
my sister and I, asleep on Valentine's eve
with bay leaves from mother's spice rack tucked beneath
our pillows? Laurel leaves brought dreams of love,
a future husband's face; or cast a spell
so in the morning the first boy we saw
would be the one. Or rose petals, laid
on next year's pillows, also conjured dreams
or spells—the books all disagreed. No dreams
of any notice came, and we forgot
our magics till the next night, discovering
the talismans in pieces in our beds.

IX.

Imagine Tituba and John Dee,
an ocean and a century between them.
Imagine them together, not in Salem
or Mortlake, but in a conjured space outside
of time and death. Barbados's umber eye
meets England's bloodshot blue, and they know themselves:
two believers ruined by their belief.
There's no need to speak or touch, but they touch,
lightly, fingertips and parted lips.
Each mirrors the other's fate, or what
they thought was fate. They feel themselves as twins,
conjoined by destiny or foolishness,
or both. Such anguished recognition is worse
than death, or the memory of death, of life
and cunning magics. It almost feels like love.

X.

I don't know why I picked this musty book
from all these walls of shelves. I'm sure its owners
never cracked the spine. By now they're deep
in canapés and Dom Perignon,
while I must mind the dog, mind the house,
take a message if anybody calls.
I'm casting deep in England, Salem, Rome.
The slow river below my borrowed view—
could that be the Tiber? Or the Thames?
Could those city lights be priestly fires?
Is pretense, a vain escape from loneliness
and lonely heart, as damning as belief?

XI.

And this, mundane until the passing of years
casts mystery upon the everyday:
an earache. Halfway through Sousa, my fingers banging
the keys to fake a difficult run, it hit,
like sudden lightning over the ocean's end.
I begged off band rehearsal and fled to the car,
not minding the heat, the leather smell
grown rank in sunshine, holding my head still.
Halfway home it vanished.

                    So, an earache.
Why this longing to read it as an omen?
Is every spotty morning nosebleed filled
with weighty portents? Should I analyze
the stubbings of my toes? The question that sets
imaginations wandering is the soft
and whispered "what if"—the threat of hazy change,
the interventions of sly devils and gods.
A word, an image, twenty year-old names,
and the mind begins its automatic game
of speculation, guessing at the lady
or tiger curled behind the sliding doors,
a different turn in a hallway, missing that flight,
a high school band rehearsal, steady flute
upheld so level, throwing back the sun,
and what on the other side? A car wreck?
A tumble down the concrete stairs? A jab
at a pudgy saxophonist that ruins her day,
provokes a binge that adds another five
contemptible pounds, depression during college,
and suicide at twenty-one? Because
my sudden earache might not have been meant
for me, or her, or anything at all.

XII.

This last poor divination into the past
must lie in memory without a name,
or none that I can find. This thumbworn book
is filled with empty words: haruspicy
from entrails, augury from flights of birds,
the Tarot, palmistry, and scrying glass.
The necromancer's future is found in death,
the numerologist's in holy math,
the tasseomancer's in a teacup's sodden leaves.
And mine? Tonight, already morning's cusp
and the new year's darkling dawn, the best
and last I have is stichomancy, the search
for fateful meaning in random pages of books.
The future's a glossary of Latin roots.

I have the benefit of history.
I see the court astrologer at work
on charts or spells, and call him a fool.
I pity Tituba her slavery,
but not her fate. The final king of Rome
may rest uneasy in Hell, regretting not
his prudence but his sudden, fearful glut.
Perhaps the demons, who relish irony,
explain the portents of their own warm guts
to eviscerated Roman and Druid priests.
Or Hell is just another prophecy,
unfounded as the rest, and all the dead
are less than dust. But I am still alive,
and cannot find myself on any page,
no hint of future, past, or present course,
no portents, omens, harbingers of life
or love, career or death in the new year.
There's nothing—or everything, too many signs
to read, interpretation overwhelmed

by meaning that swoops and swirls through every word
and image—bleeding roadkill, shapes in clouds,
a random, channel-surfing sentence voiced
by twenty throats.

                  The dog upstairs can't rest;
her collar jingles down to me. I climb
the spiral steps and find her waiting there.
She noses my palm. Before the window's view
we sit, her bearish head in my lap, and watch
the lights wink out and fade on either side
of the black and still Ohio. The night gives way
to utter dark, and the sun is slow to rise.

III

NOCCALULA FALLS

They've made a park of it,
a trail bordered by dusty marigolds
leading to the falls, a respectable stream
tumbling over good Alabama marble—
more expensive than Italian, we're told—
frothing white for an instant,
then down the Coosa to Gadsden.

Water is water. More interesting, the polished plaque:

how the Indian princess, Noccalula,
rather than marry at her father's command,
threw herself over the falls,
which he named for her in grief.

Even as visitors snap at the words,
something uneasy filters in,
even as the zoo's one shabby lion
behind two circles of chain-link
looms so dark and obsolete
that the developed shot will hold only outline
and the glint of an eye—

even then something is a lie
in history and its telling.
We've reinvented romance in the wilderness,
a tragic tableau waiting to be engraved
and sold in London penny-dreadfuls,
sold to us now, here, paid for
by grim Andrew Jackson on the twenty-dollar bill.

We have the names, rolling syllables
older than maps:
Tuscaloosa, Etowah,
Choccolocco, Talladega, Cheaha,
Noccalula,
princess of ghosts.

FEASTING

In Alabama we joke that possums
are born dead on a highway. In truth,
they're slow and stupid, drawn by the stink
of what's already dead, a cat or squirrel
or another cannibal possum,
crushed and melting to grease in the sun.
One carcass spawns many,
and my swervings grow wilder until I drive
like a drunk to avoid their bones.

Possum eats dog eats coon eats rat,
and crow eats them all.
When my swooping lights catch them
at their feasts, my eyes meet theirs,
red-reflected, and I have to guess in a second
which way they will run. I twist
the wheel, brace for the thump,
check all the mirrors for a shape
humping into the grass or lying still.
The next day, the crows, ripping
and gorging, wait until the last instant
to flutter gracelessly away,
already returning as I pass.

A VISION IN GEORGIA

Through morning fog drifting to shore
as if from a fire on the other side,
I saw a bird whose name, *sandhill crane,*
appeared in my mouth like a ghost.

A brushstroke inked on rice paper,
scented with jasmine tea, the crane posed
like an S in the gray light,
its unimagined feet lost in the water.
It did not look at me, but at the river
pooled around its tapered legs,
carrying its reflection back to Savannah,
Honshu, a black drop in a brush,
the country of its birth.

THE RETIRED WELDER TURNS TO GARDENING

He's gentler now. His swollen hands that worked
on almost every dam in Alabama,
bending steel to fit the concrete seams,
now cradle seeds. His fingers poke the holes
in dirt made rich with cow manure; they drop
the seeds and bury them snug; they pull the weeds;
they pinch tobacco worms from ripe tomatoes.
In younger days his fingers knew the tricks
of prying bottle caps and winding tight
his belt around his fist as the boy stood by,
waiting for his licks. His pitching arm
could lob a whiskey bottle eighty feet,
and he loved the laughing sound of shattered glass
almost as much as his torch's private hum.
Now he no longer loves those things.
The garden, sloping down a hundred feet
to overlook the K-Mart and Dairy Queen,
is mostly meant to fill his table: peas,
zucchini, crookneck squash, collard greens,
a fig tree, okra tapering like knives.
He's generous with what he grows, although
his son looks bemused at the sacks of greens,
and rolls his eyes at boiling them with hamhocks.
The boy (he cannot help but think of him
as still a boy) prefers his fig preserves.
The old man brings collards anyway.

While he loves his garden's fruits, still more
he loves the oddities. He keeps a patch
of scrubby cotton to show his granddaughters,
plucking bolls and guiding their fingertips
through fibrous clouds to the sticky seeds within.
His sunflowers turn their showy heads and nod,
obedient to the bruised and jet-streaked dusk.
The gourds he hangs from twine, stretching out

their necks, twisting them around poles,
bending not with fire now but time.
As he walks between the rows, the stray cats
he feeds all gather at his heels and follow,
their greedy purrs subdued to background murmur.
The children, the boy and his girls, don't come as much
as he would like, but every time he shows
them how to feel the cotton seeds, and gives
each one a dried-out gourd with a corkscrew neck.
He's gentler now, more patient. The things he loves
will bend to him no more with fire, but time.

IN THE SHADOWS

The leather case, slim in my palm, could carry lipstick.
Capsaicin stream fires up to six feet,
with marking dye for identification.
One night, here beside the Hebrew College
in Cincinnati, a man ran from behind
and blocked the sidewalk, saying, "Wait!
I want to ask you a question!" I kept walking;
he backed up, still blocking, saying "Wait!"
"What?" I asked, pulling the spray from my pocket,
my thumb poised to slide from safety and shoot.
He held his hands up, fingers spread,
saying "No, no, nevermind," and backed away.
I don't know what he wanted—money, directions?
But this is America, a city, and a woman alone at night.
I would have used it, aimed straight for the eyes,
kept firing until he was on his knees
and kicked him in the head for good measure.

This is the image the manufacturers have dreamed,
or culled from our dreams, photographed
and packaged: a shadowy man hiding
in the bushes, the empty parking lot,
the empty echoing stairwell,
some figment slow and clumsy enough
to be brought down by a pepper spritz.

Real shadows rise up at my side.
No one, the second shadow my own.
Passing a streetlight, another appears; I am three,
I am four, me and all my darkling casts.

DESCRIBING DEER TO A BLIND WOMAN IN SEWANEE, TENNESSEE

There are three of them, two does and a fawn.
They stand in the shade, nibbling at the grass,
angling their heads to watch us while they eat.

Does? They're smaller than bucks, no antlers.
The fawn is even smaller, not much bigger
than your dog. It's golden brown like caramel
with white spots in rows on its flanks.

Brown? It's the smell of dirt in your garden
on hot afternoons. Gold is the sound
of cymbals clashing. White is empty and clean; it can be beautiful
or terrifying, hot or cold, and it smells and tastes like ice.

The does eat cautiously, never taking their eyes
from us, even as they curve their necks
to the grass. The fawn walks fearlessly between the does,
careless of motherhood. Its uncertain hooves
are blurred with tender green.

But the words are only metaphors;
I can't spell for you their color, their grace,
the simple wonder of deer in a park.
Language is a crutch. Lean on it
with all our weight, as much as it can bear.